W9-BTR-220

CHILLY CHARLIE

By Dana Meachen Rau

Illustrated by Martin Lemelman

Children's Press®
A Division of Grolier Publishing
New York • London • Hong Kong • Sydney
Danbury, Connecticut

FOR THE REAL CHARLIE
—D. M. R.

FOR SAM
—M. L.

Reading Consultant
Katharine A. Kane
Education Consultant
(Retired, San Diego County Office of Education
and San Diego State University)

Visit Children's Press® on the Internet at:
http://publishing.grolier.com

Library of Congress Cataloging-in-Publication Data
Rau, Dana Meachen.
    Chilly Charlie / by Dana Meachen Rau; illustrated by Martin Lemelman.
       p. cm. — (Rookie reader)
    Summary: Charlie is chilly all over and needs a hug to warm him up.
    ISBN 0-516-22210-4 (lib. bdg.)   0-516-27288-8 (pbk.)
    [1. Cold—Fiction. 2. Hugging—Fiction. 3. Stories in rhyme.] I. Lemelman,
Martin, ill. II. Title. III. Series.
PZ8.3.R232Ch   2001
[E]—dc21   00-038427

GROLIER
PUBLISHING

Charlie is
always chilly,

3

on his fingers,

on his toes.

He is chilly on his elbows,

on his cheeks,

and on his nose.

How can Charlie warm up?

Drink cocoa in a mug?

Wrap up in a blanket?

No!

Charlie needs a hug!

Word List (27 words)

a	drink	mug
always	elbows	needs
and	fingers	no
blanket	he	nose
can	his	on
Charlie	how	toes
cheeks	hug	up
chilly	in	warm
cocoa	is	wrap

About the Author

Dana Meachen Rau is the author of many books for children, including historical fiction, storybooks, biographies, and numerous books in the Rookie Reader series. She also works as an illustrator and editor. When she's not busily typing on her computer or buried in piles of paper, she drinks cocoa with her husband, Chris, and son, Charlie, in Farmington, Connecticut.

About the Illustrator

Martin Lemelman is busy living his second childhood in Allentown, Pennsylvania, with his wife, Monica, and his four sons (all art critics). He has created illustrations for many magazines and children's books. He is also a professor in the Communications Design Department at Kutztown University. This is his first book for Children's Press.